FAIL POINT

THE REAL REASON MARRIAGES BREAK DOWN... AND HOW YOU CAN START TO TURN IT AROUND

MARRIAGE FAIL POINT

THE REAL REASON MARRIAGES BREAK DOWN... AND HOW YOU CAN START TO TURN IT AROUND

By

LEE H. BAUCOM, PH.D.

LeeBaucom.com

TABLE OF CONTENTS

INTRODUCTION

I'm betting you are not reading this book for fun. Unless you are just very curious, you are here for an important reason: your marriage.

Maybe you have realized that something is wrong in your marriage, but you are not clear what. Or perhaps your spouse has made it painfully clear that something is very wrong with your marriage and you fear the worst. Either way, my guess is that you are not here for a fun read.

My task is pretty straightforward. It is to help you begin to move through the current mess to something better — a marriage you both will treasure. And in this book, my particular task is to help you understand what happened, to explain why your marriage got into trouble — and to point you toward help. Secondarily, I want to help you begin to move forward to a better marriage.

What happened is far less important than what you do now. While it is important to understand what happened and why it happened, the critical thing is getting to a better relationship.

Before we even begin, let me commend you. Every marriage has problems (I will remind you about that again in a later chapter). Not every couple resolves the problems. About half give up and divorce. Remember that not every person involved in a hurting marriage decides to try and figure this out. Many simply fold and walk away.

But you are here. You are trying.

And I am here to help you with that process.

We know why you are here. So just briefly, I want to tell you why I am here. I have been helping save marriages for three decades now. Over the last couple of decades, I have had the opportunity to help couples around the world. I've coached and taught many couples to get to a healthy spot, often from the verge of divorce. I have also had the pleasure of teaching many relationship coaches my principles, allowing them to help even more couples.

But the beginning of my work is in my childhood. I was fortunate to have had happily married parents. I never had a doubt about the stability of my family as I grew up. I knew my parents would stay married. It was just an assumption.

While that was true for me, I watched my cousins who did not have that advantage. I watched the devastation divorces caused as they ripped through my extended family. I realized, even then, that divorce had an emotional impact on children. But I also saw the emotional devastation to the adults. It was painful to watch, even with my limited understanding as a child.

In college, I first learned to understand the family as a system, a pattern of interactions linking all members of that family together. And it was in that moment that I understood why the divorces had been so devastating. It ripped the fabric of family relationships into tatters, pulling at every single person involved.

As I worked toward my graduate degrees, and finally, a Ph.D., I studied how to best help families and couples in trouble. And with my newly minted degrees, I began to work with couples, just as I had been taught... and I noticed a disconcerting lack of success.

Was it me? Was I just a bad therapist?

Or was it something else?

I began to do some extra research... outside of the areas of my grad school learning. And I unearthed some shocking statistics on just how poorly therapy was helping couples.

According to meta-studies of the research, about half of couples who go to therapy end up divorced — just about the same as for the general population. Only 10 to 15 percent of couples reported any help or improvement from the therapy. About 5 out of every 10 couples who go to therapy still divorce. And only 1 in 10 said they improved.

Shocking, right? Given that therapy is the first line of defense to help troubled marriages, I was horrified and outraged! We were failing marriages... while marriages were failing!

I began trying some different strategies. I tested and explored. I got extra training, including extensive training as a life coach. I refined and taught my approach. And I created an online program, the Save The Marriage System, so couples anywhere could get help at any time.

Since that time, I have continued to work with couples on every continent (except, to date, Antarctica) to turn their broken marriages around.

But more than that, I have also helped individuals work on their relationships, even when their spouse showed no interest in trying... or even was resolved to divorce.

You see, humans tend to be very binary in crisis thinking. Either this or that. No other options. "Either we stay married, or we get divorced." A or B. We can't see that there is a "third option" of working on the marriage and healing it.

But guess what? Many times, there IS a Third Option. There **is** a way to get to the marriage you both would treasure (and protect). You might not be able to see it from here.

Take my word for it. I've seen it happen, in case after case, for decades.

And it can happen for you, too.

But first, we need to clarify what happened and why it happened. That is the purpose of this book. It is a quick but crucial read.

ABOUT THIS BOOK

My purpose in writing this book is simply to help you understand what happened in your marriage. We will discuss the difference between the symptoms of your problems (which many people confuse as the cause of their problems) and the true cause(s) of your marital crisis. Confusing the two keeps you chasing after the wrong thing, "solving" one symptom, only for another to appear. "Whack-A-Mole" is not an efficient or helpful way to solve a crisis.

We will discuss the importance of connection, the role it plays, and the effects of disconnection, so you understand the heart of the crisis. And then, it will become crystal clear how your marriage got into trouble. Most of the time (like, almost every single time), it is a matter of neglect, not maliciousness. (Understand that the actions of a spouse can feel malicious. But those actions are more often out of hurt and pain. See the note below, though.)

And we will spend some time answering questions people commonly have at this stage. My task is to speak directly to you, to make sure you are clear on what happened (and why) and point you toward resolution/healing of your marriage.

Which will be my last area — how to get help for your marriage. While the scope of this book is the question of why your marriage got into trouble, you also want to know the next steps. The problem is that many people try to jump to the steps, without figuring out why they are where they are. If I am lost, out in the middle of nowhere, and I call for help, there is a fundamental question — "Where ARE you?" If you don't know where you are, it is very difficult to plot a course to where you want to be.

So, we start with discovering why your marriage got into trouble.

SPECIAL NOTE: As I said just a few paragraphs back, neglect is often the cause of problems. I noted that people are not malicious as much as responding from hurt. Their hurt can feel hurtful because it comes out in anger.

That said, this is no reason or excuse for abusive behavior. If your spouse is physically threatening or hurting you, this is not the time to try to "figure it out." This is the time for you to find safety. Abuse often escalates. It is also founded on control and domination.

This makes it impossible to work toward a mutual relationship. An abusive person is trying to control, not to partner. Your safety is far more important than the relationship.

If you find yourself in an abusive relationship, please stop reading RIGHT NOW and get help for yourself and any children. You need to be safe. And you do not deserve to be hurt (the same is true for your children).

If you have been or are being hurt, please contact the domestic violence hotline and get help: 1-800-799-7233 (TTY 1-800-787-3224) or contact your local domestic violence shelter.

If you are continuing to read, it is my assumption that your marriage is not an abusive one... simply a hurting one. So, let's get busy with understanding why this happened so that you can get to a better place in your relationship.

LEGAL NOTES

The purpose of this book is to educate and clarify why relationships have issues. The specific focus is the marital relationship.

Any information included should not be construed as a substitute for professional help. If your marriage is in trouble and in need of help, you should pursue any help necessary.

The author is not providing legal or medical advice on any particular situation, nor should it be construed as such.

The reader is responsible for deciding how the information applies to his or her particular situation.

By deciding to read the material, the reader is assuming responsibility and risk for his or her own situation.

CHAPTER 1.

A SHORT GUIDE TO WHY MARRIAGES GET IN TROUBLE

Sarah was in tears, choking back the tears. She told me her husband had just revealed how unhappy he was. He told her that a divorce was the only resolution he could see. He told her he just couldn't do it anymore.

It happens just about every day. I speak to someone, get an email or message from someone. And just like Sarah, it starts with "I had no idea," and continues on with the shock of discovering their spouse was either unhappy and struggling or unhappy and ready to leave. They conclude with "I didn't see it coming! What can I do?"

Sarah told me that she knew their relationship was not good. She just thought it was a "phase," and that it would get better. That is often true for people. But sometimes, people aren't even clear that the marriage is hurting, and that their spouse isn't happy. They are surprised when their spouse reveals both the unhappiness and the desire to end the relationship.

As we talked, Sarah had questions: What happened? What caused the marriage crisis? Why did it get so bad? And does it have to end the relationship? More importantly, is there another way through the crisis than divorce?

Years ago, during my training days, it was that first client who told me that he had no idea that his marriage was even in trouble. He was genuinely shocked and dismayed that his wife was A) unhappy, B) wanting a divorce, and C) already dating someone else.

I was shocked that he was shocked! How had he not known, I wondered?

Over and over, I heard the same story in my office time and again. Person after person was surprised by how deeply their marriage was hurting, and how an unhappy spouse was quickly becoming a bitter spouse.

In those early days, I just assumed that in such an intimate relationship as marriage, if the connection was on the decline, both people would feel and know it. Both people, I had assumed, would be unhappy and aware of the other spouse's unhappiness.

I was wrong.

And now, all these years later, I am clear on why a spouse misses the looming crisis (or at least isn't paying attention), and why the crisis started in the first place.

It is pretty much "baked into" the culture of marriage we have created. And It happens far too frequently, given the fact that family is the fabric of society. The way families go is the way society goes.

Fractured families lead to fractured society. Which is why saving marriages is so important. And given the pain involved, it is why saving your marriage is so important.

Let's first take a quick look at how this all starts, and then we will see where it often gets into trouble (and why).

"We're Engaged!" (...And So It Begins)

In another chapter, I discuss the process of connection (and disconnection), since that is the heart of any marital relationship (really, the lifeblood of the relationship). But first, let's just peek behind what happens for most couples.

At first, there are just two people, doing their thing, living life. Then... they meet, the two of them, and there is just something there. Something special.

Special enough that both people push the relationship along, becoming more and more serious over time. They proclaim their love for each other as they express their love for each other. Each works to make the other feel the love. And their relationship grows.

And one day, they decide to get married. Given social media, these moments have become quite the event. But in reality, it is two people deciding and agreeing to join their lives together — they just don't really know what that means yet (and many never quite figure it out).

Fast forward to the wedding. It may take place in a church, at the courthouse, in a garden, on a beach, or at some other destination. But the soul of that service is still the same: two people pledging to love each other and keep all others outside of their relationship, for life. They legally join together as an entity, as a couple, and they go on their way.

I remember that moment so clearly in my own life. I walked into that church, single. Perhaps 40 minutes later, we emerged from that church, married — a couple! I was the same person, but something had changed. It took years for me to figure out the shift that was underway.

In our culture, I don't think we are prepared for marriage. Many couples get married with little to no preparation for the marital relationship (although the wedding, itself, gets lots of attention). In our case, my spouse and I did attend some pre-marital counseling sessions. Other couples may have to attend pre-marital counseling, a workshop, or a weekend retreat. But that is usually the extent of the training most of us get. And then, we are married. After that, all the training is "on the job."

The problem is, most couples believe they have already beaten divorce! They think that they are not going to have problems, that their love will see them through, and that others don't have what they have.

How do I know? Because that was my own experience... and because I spent the better part of 20 years providing pre-marital counseling for a number of churches in my area. If someone was going to get married at any of six local churches, they had to come through my office.

Earnest and hopeful, they all believed that they were the exceptions. Sure, they knew there might be some problems, but nothing that their love wouldn't get them through.

Think about that for a moment. Given divorce statistics, they were stepping into a situation that, statistically speaking, had the odds of a coin toss. Nearly half of marriages end in divorce. And yet, couples bravely (and/or naively) get married, believing that those statistics do not apply to them.

When I was learning to drive a car, I spent an entire school semester in driving class. I had to log hours of supervised driving. And I had to prove to the state that I knew enough about driving to deserve a driver's license.

Interestingly, given the importance of marriage, in most situations, a marriage license costs just a few dollars and only requires a few signatures. And instantly, you are tied together, legally speaking and without further legal intervention, for life.

Most couples enter into marriage with very little preparation or knowledge.

How about you?

Let's say that your parents didn't have a great marriage. Perhaps you even knew they weren't happy. So that wasn't a great model for you. Or maybe they divorced (which, statistically speaking, would be true about half of the time), so that was the model you had.

Or maybe you were fortunate and came from a happy family, your parents happily married. The secrets of a happy couple reside behind closed doors and in their own minds. You don't get to see it. You may be able to see how they treat each other in public. But so much of a successful marriage is invisible from the outside.

You miss their moments of connection, and their methods of dealing with disconnection. So, in essence, you don't even get great models there. You only see the evidence of a marriage being happy. You can only speculate on how they got there.

So it is, two people walk into their wedding ceremony, loving each other and pledging to do that for life. And they walk out a couple. People pat them on the back, hug and congratulate them, and send them out to face the world together.

Sound familiar?

It should. It's the story of the start of marriage for most people. They are running more on love, an earnest desire for it to work, and commitment, than on knowledge and know-how.

Is love important? Absolutely.

Is commitment important? More than anything.

Do people know what they mean? And how to do those things? Nope. Not at all.

And that is the tragedy. Marriages end because people don't understand what they are doing in the beginning. And from there, they either stumble into an approach that works, or they fall apart. (Many stay together. But some only stay in the legal shell of marriage.)

Crucial Shift: You/Me to *WE*

Before a relationship starts, there are just two people, unconnected. Then, they meet. And at some point, either instantly or after a bit, those two people realize that there is something different here... an attraction, a connection.

At that moment, there is a "You" and a "Me" — "You seem interesting to me, and I would like to know more about you." And they begin spending more time with each other, doing what they can to increase the connection.

"You and Me" begins to be an understanding... a relationship. They start having feelings for each other and take actions to demonstrate that feeling. And those actions also serve to intensify the feelings.

Actions lead to feelings that lead to actions that lead to feelings that lead to actions that lead to feelings.

At some point, the connection is so strong that they call it "love." This confusing mass of emotions and desires is so powerful that they just can't not be together. And "You and Me" decide to make it permanent; they decide to pledge their lives together, to join together, in a committed relationship, for the rest of their lives.

Often, in our culture, they decide to marry and begin a life together, just the two of them. But they still imagine "You and Me" doing it together.

Perhaps they thought marriage was "just the next thing to do," having dated for some internally important time or because of some external event or deadline. Or maybe they just want to make sure they won't lose that person. Or perhaps they are so "in love" that they want to sustain that feeling forever (or at least for life).

There are lots of justifications and reasons people use to explain what they chose to do (many people negatively recall the decision and the reasons behind it when their marriage is in crisis). But in the end, they make a pledge/promise/commitment to be together, as a unit, for the rest of their lives, promising to keep any threat to that relationship away.

More than that, they promise that this is a "no matter what" promise, including times when they are healthy or sick, when they are prosperous or poor, when things are going well or even when things aren't going well at all. They pledge to persevere and get through it together.

And yet, nearly half of all marriages in the United States do not fulfill that pledge.

Why?

In large part, because they do not make a shift... a crucial shift. They do not ever shift from "You and Me" to *WE*.

Why not?

Because most people do not realize that this is necessary — even critical — in a marriage. Major religions have described it as "two becoming one flesh." But many (probably most) people do not consider what that means (or how to do it). And so, they never make the shift.

Which leads to a destructive path — "You and Me" becomes "You vs. Me." If they don't begin the shift to *WE*, they begin a struggle. A power struggle, in part. An identity struggle, for sure.

The destruction of a marriage is rooted in that struggle. And it is activated because two people do not understand the necessary shift.

One major cause of your marriage crisis? You did not become a *WE*.

The *WE*

When couples become a *WE*, it does not mean that they will never have a conflict again and that things are smooth sailing. In fact, notice that our wedding vows both commit to becoming a *WE* and persevering through any type of days life throws our way — better days and worse days.

It's just that a couple who becomes a *WE* perseveres through those tough times by standing together as a team, a unit. They see that they are now indivisible, forever joined. They have each other's back, they are a team... but even more deeply, they are a unit.

That is exactly how the government views marriage. It is a new entity, to be seen as a unit, not as individuals. Assets are joint, owned by the *WE*. Children "belong" to both. Taxes can be filed for this unit — as a unit. That marriage license was a legal contract for creating this new *WE*.

But where else does this happen in life? Nowhere. So no wonder we don't know that is what we are doing! We have no training. For most of our lives, we are raised as individuals. Part of a family, sure. But responsible for ourselves. We spend our childhood, adolescence, and often, a part of adulthood, looking out for "Me."

Then, with that simple ceremony, we join into a *WE*.

But only if we know that is what *WE* are doing.

And most people don't.

This is the "hidden" part of marriage — and the critical part. Maybe your parents had a great marriage because they forged a *WE*. But since lots of being a *WE* are in the perceptions and mindset of the individuals, you didn't see it. You might miss the actions that show that *WE*. So, you didn't know what was happening.

Or maybe your parents didn't know that was the goal, either. They were stumbling through marriage (or divorce) without knowing this was the key.

Either way, unless you figured it out, you likely missed the critical shift in becoming a *WE*.

So first, let me clarify this: becoming a *WE* does not lessen the individuals involved. It is not about being a "superglue" relationship, so tightly bound that you have to lose your own individuality to join in.

In fact, becoming a great *WE* requires two individuals showing up with their best selves. They bring their gifts and abilities to the *WE*. They just choose to join together with another person to face the world... knowing you are in it together, bringing your resources to each other in order to get there.

For an incredibly rough analogy, consider an athletic team. The team members are working toward a common goal — winning. And the way to win? By playing at your best. You practice and condition, so you are ready for the game. Then, you bring your best self and your best abilities to the game... as do your teammates.

Sure, it is possible for someone to let their ego get in the way, to "hog the ball" and keep others from playing their best game. But that is because they don't yet realize the power of a team, versus the limits of an individual. The team is a group of individuals, joining together for a common goal. And part of that goal is helping all the other players perform at their best, while also playing at their best. But those connections go beyond just a common goal. It is a sense of purpose and connection — *WE* win together!

Since we are using analogies, let me give another very rough analogy. In the legal and business world, there is the legal entity of the "corporation." Even that word tells you something. It is from the Latin *corporare*, which means "combine in one body."

Let's say that you have an idea for a new business. But you want to build it into something bigger than just you. So, you decide to "incorporate." You fill out legal forms, file them with the state, and you have created an imaginary entity — the "corporation." There is, at that moment, nothing to it. It exists on paper and in a legal sense. But it is mostly in the mind and mindset. (Much like that marriage license and the wedding that officially forms the union.)

But over time, you treat the corporation like it is real. You may have a headquarters — a home. Accounting procedures are done for the "corporation." You talk about "the company," and it begins to become more and more real. Until it becomes a unit, a real entity.

The same is true of the marriage. The more you see the entity of *WE*, the more you treat it as real, the more you make decisions based on *WE*, the more it becomes real.

Why No *WE*?

If *WE* is a basic requirement for a prospering and loving marriage, why doesn't it happen? Why don't more marriages get there?

There are many reasons. We have already pointed to one: a lack of awareness. People simply do not know that they are supposed to do that. They do not know they are moving toward a new relationship and a new entity. So, they resist the process, fearing they will lose themselves.

And part of that resistance is also due to our ego. We don't want to lose control of our lives, and we don't want to need someone else. We should "stand on our own two feet!"

Those messages about "doing your own thing," "taking care of yourself," and similar messages of individuality are in the fabric of our culture. And those cultural messages can keep us stuck in the individualistic model. More than that, those cultural messages revolve around the "cult of the ego," that the rugged individual is the way to be.

And so, in many marriages, two people keep saying, "you do your thing, and I will do mine." Keeping them stuck in "You and Me," and eventually, in "You versus Me."

The fuel behind this stubborn hold on ME is the other piece of the puzzle. It is fear. It fuels the process. Interestingly, there are actually two fears that really get in the way.

The "fear of intimacy" is directly tied to that place of being a ME. The fear of intimacy is really the fear of losing yourself (your distinctiveness, your self-determination, your sense of self) to the relationship. The fear of intimacy is the fear of really letting someone in, letting them really know you, and giving them some say-so in your life.

So, in an attempt to preserve the self and fight the fear, people push and rebel against the natural pull toward *WE* that comes in the marriage.

But since we have that deep need for connection — particularly with one person — we suffer another, almost opposite, fear. That is the "fear of abandonment." We fear losing the relationship (and the person) that we feel we need to be okay and secure. So, we grab at that person, holding them tight, while not being at our best self.

These two fears, both unconscious, tend to push against each other. And here is the thing: we all have both fears within us. We all can operate from either fear. More than that, each fear can trigger the other.

If I fear intimacy, I might pull away, triggering my spouse's fear of abandonment, leading to my spouse trying to pull me closer. Which serves to heighten my fear of intimacy, leading me to pull further away, leading my spouse to have deeper fears of abandonment, trying to pull me even closer.

If I fear abandonment, I try to pull my spouse closer, triggering a fear of intimacy, leading my spouse to pull away, deepening my fear of abandonment, causing me to try even harder to pull my spouse closer, deepening my spouse's fear of intimacy, leading to further distancing.

One fear triggers the other. And both spouses have both fears. It is baked into us.

While both people have both fears, many people have a more dominant fear. One of the two is more easily triggered, often due to other experiences in life... all the way back to childhood. That fear is more easily triggered. But if a spouse reverses course and moves to the other fear, it will often trigger the opposite fear in a spouse.

In the process, the couple gets into a tug-of-war... all based on fears that are neither useful nor actual. We can be close to someone without losing ourselves. And we can be okay, in spite of losing a relationship. It just doesn't feel that way when a fear is triggered.

Knowing what fear is being triggered can help you to decide how to respond (versus reacting). Fear does not have to choose our actions. It can be background noise, and we can still choose our actions. Which, ironically, calms the fears. Often, for both people.

Quick Summary

Marriages are designed to be a relationship of *WE*, of being a team, connected and looking out for what is best for the relationship. It is not a loss of identity, but an opportunity to bring the best self to the best union.

But since we don't know that is the goal, and lack the experience in getting there, we often miss the goal. And when we miss the goal, we shift to You vs. Me, struggling over identity and control.

In the process, we trigger fears that further erode the connection, leading us to relate fearfully. Which places both people on the defensive, making the connection more tenuous and disconnected.

Unless one or both people recognize this pattern, the relating becomes so painful that one or both decide to dissolve the relationship — in the hopes of stopping the pain.

Ironically, breaking the unconscious bond of *WE*, no matter how tenuous that bond, is incredibly painful. The pain of the relationship becomes an incredibly painful dissolution of the relationship. What seemed like a solution only leads to further pain.

Unless the couple finds a way through, and back to *WE*.

The danger, though, is that we rely on our emotional state to chart a course. Let's talk about "just not feeling it" in the next chapter.

CHAPTER 2.

"I JUST DON'T FEEL IT!"

"I love you, but I'm not 'in love' with you" is the start of many a relationship talk... and marks the spiraling of a marriage that has been in free-fall for a while.

It may be proclaiming, "I just don't feel the way I should." Or "I'm just not happy." Different expressions for the same reality — something is NOT right in the marriage that words don't adequately express. Primarily, because the one saying them cannot quite make sense of them, either.

And yet, the spiral accelerates downward.

Is there a way to recover from this? Yes. But only when you more fully understand what happened and why.

We have already discussed one issue: WE was never created. It is not so much about "achieved" as "created" or "formed," since WE is a natural shift... when we quit fighting and avoiding it.

Along the way, though, something else shifts. Call it passion, call it "chemistry," call it attraction. That pull toward someone that is magnetic and electric... at least at the beginning of a relationship.

And then, something happened.

We might remember that time at the beginning. You wanted to be together all the time. Maybe you just couldn't keep your hands off each other. Butterflies were more like bats in your stomach when you anticipated seeing your beloved. The attraction was so strong. And you thought it would never go away.

Until it did.

Connection fuels that attraction in the beginning. But this is also a biochemical reality. And that reality is unsustainable. (Which is probably for the best, given the obsessive nature of that level of attraction. Life, as exciting as it feels, is mostly suspended during this time. Available energy is focused on the love and the person.)

This stage of the relationship is about infatuation — the overwhelming attraction and connection to the other person that leaves both people in a state of arousal and desire.

It is powerful. It is frightening. It is fun. It is exciting. And it is unsustainable. The body and brain simply cannot keep up with the biochemical state. Eventually, the brain gets used to that state... and begins to return to the baseline.

Did anything happen in the relationship to cause this? No. It is a biological shift. But it can leave one or both people confused. Or cause one or both people to shift away, even walk away.

Author and marriage expert, Gary Chapman calls those feelings of infatuation "the tingles." According to Chapman, research shows that this stage is not sustainable in a relationship beyond about 18 months. But during that period, you are so "in love," that you tend to show your love in every conceivable way. To use his idea, you speak every language of love you can! (You can listen to my interview with Gary Chapman here: https://savethemarriage.com/lovelanguage)

Biochemically, the author and therapist Bob Grant, points out, you are shifting from an "adrenaline attraction" to an "endorphin attraction." The shift is not indicative of the failure of the relationship. It is really a natural and necessary shift to a new level. And actually, a higher level.

In the early days of a relationship, excitement rules. Adrenaline fuels it. There may be some excitement over the newness of things — discovering each other and learning about each other. There is also some fear that fuels the excitement: "What if he/she does not feel the same?" "What if she/he finds someone else?" "What if I mess this up?" "What can I do to hold onto this person?"

Two elements swirl together, attraction and excitement. And the outcome is that adrenaline attraction. The hopes and fears, the physical connection, causes the body/brain to stay in overdrive... desperate to be together and stay together.

Then, you add in the commitment. You make promises to stay together and work through things that come up. You solidify the relationship... and remove some of the fears. And at the same time, your body and brain are beginning to stop reacting to the same adrenaline shots. The body begins to return to normal, and the brain is no longer hijacked from the chemical cocktail.

Life returns to normal. And the relationship has the potential of growing to a new level.

Unless you confuse this shift with a loss of love.

You see, we tend to confuse infatuation with love. "I've never felt this way" is the proof. What we miss is that the infatuation is part of the bonding process... but not indicative of love. It is indicative of a physiological response to the new connection.

And the connection remains when the physical state returns to normal... unless one or both members of the relationship are fooled into believing the infatuation WAS the love.

Reality television and affairs both demonstrate that the feelings of infatuation can come between people, given the right triggering circumstances, and not really be love but chemical. (Don't believe me? Take a look at how many Bachelor/Bachelorette relationships actually sustain past the show. The same is true of affairs. Most affairs also fizzle. In spite of — in both cases — a person proclaiming, "I found the love of my life.")

But love sustains through the infatuation and into the shift — adrenaline to endorphin.

In your body, adrenaline and endorphins can both make you feel good. Adrenaline is triggered by what is happening TO you. Endorphins are triggered by what you are DOING. Adrenaline has elements of fear. Endorphins are more about safety.

Now you see how that shift fits into the relationship. And why it can be a better place. When there is adrenaline, there is uncertainty and risk. You might just lose that person!

When there are endorphins, there is certainty and commitment. You are loving the person who is loving you. Both have committed to being there.

Which is why some people, when things get too stable, stir things up. They are trying to get the fix of adrenaline.

Grabbing At Infatuation

It's easy to get rather addicted to the adrenaline present in the infatuation stage. Some people want that excitement and arousal. So, whenever things start to calm down — when things begin to solidify, and commitments are made — they pull back and stir uncertainty back into the relationship. That shift can feel exciting to the individual. But it is stressful to the relationship. Over time, the drama stresses and breaks the relationship.

Such people are chasing the kick of adrenaline. It is a rather addictive substance that our own body creates. Many "adrenaline junkies" fulfill that need with exciting sports activities, scary movies, or amusement park rides. But others find it in relationship excitement. One of their reasons for a relationship is to get their fix of adrenaline.

When a motivator for connecting is adrenaline, whenever the adrenaline drops (the relationship is no longer as exciting), they either leave or create drama in the relationship. This, though, is not common — except for the common misunderstanding that relationships should be exciting... or something is wrong.

Why do people mistake the adrenaline-spiked infatuation with love? Because it is the picture we are fed by television, books, and movies. We are sold that the romantic excitement of infatuation is the hallmark of love. It's not just a stage of a relationship, but the real thing!

Then, when it wanes, they panic and doubt the relationship. Some simply flee in fear they will "never feel it again" with that same person. And so, from that person's perspective, the shift in the relationship is not growth but failure.

When we rely on the adrenaline to "feel love," there is often nothing left for love when the adrenaline finally abates (and it does). The connection has been too stressed by the chasing after adrenaline. The relationship can become exhausted and stressed.

But perhaps equally important, sometimes, people fail to move toward love when the infatuation cools.

Shifting To Endorphins

Some sense the shift, accept that things have changed... but don't know what to do now. Love feels different. But they don't have the skills to keep it nurtured.

The infatuation stage can feel like that rollercoaster ride. Slow anxiety-provoking climbs, exciting drops, and bucking turns. Exciting? Yes.

Exhausting? Yes.

And mostly automatic.

It "just happens." No need to force it. You just feel it, and go with it. Which is why people often say things like, "There is no explaining it. We just fell in love. It was so natural and easy. No work. We just clicked."

You almost can't help it.

And you can't help the shift from adrenaline to endorphins. It, too, is a natural process.

But sustaining the love — that is a different matter.

At this point, love is not the romantic feeling, the ache for being with the beloved. It is based on love, the verb. It is about acting in love. Taking action to be loving. Which does not diminish the love. It simply means that now, love is conscious, a choice, and a commitment.

It is also sustainable... unless you don't sustain it.

When people ask the secret of sustainable love, it is two people committed to being a *WE*, acting lovingly toward each other. They stay connected and loving.

And by leading with loving action, they continue to feel the love. Acting on love leads to feeling in love.

Until the actions stop.

Is the feeling of "in love" gone? No. It is fueled, though, by the connection now. It is fueled by "doing" love, not just feeling it. The actions of being loving lead to connection. And the connection leads to feeling in love. The intensity is different but no less real. In fact, more real. It is no longer based on a runaway (but unsustainable) process, but a sustainable and nurtured love — one that can last a lifetime.

When The Shift Failed

Many marriages fail because a couple fails to navigate the shift from adrenaline to endorphins, from infatuation to love. The ingredients were there, but they didn't shift. Many times, this is simply the fact that the couple did not recognize the shift was natural and necessary.

Just to be clear, the shift may happen long before marriage. They managed to start the shift, but they didn't maintain it. They started to become concerned that "something is wrong." They know they "love" this other person, but they "don't feel it."

The adrenaline waned, so the heat cooled a bit. And with the cool, the couple assumes that something is drastically wrong. And so, they pull away from each other. Which leaves more distance and less fuel. It should then not be much of a surprise when even more "coolness" comes to the relationship. Less conscious connection leads to more doubt and less motivation. Which leads to more disconnection. And the cycle continues.

Unless...

Unless or until one person decides to act. Because disconnection tends to be automatic. But it is not unavoidable. There is the conscious choice to act on love. To move toward a spouse, act lovingly, and rebuild the connection.

This is an important point: "acting lovingly" is not about faking it. It is about taking loving — conscious — actions toward a spouse. It isn't about being caught up in "I'm just not feeling it" beliefs; it is knowing and understanding that love is in action. And acting lovingly leads to loving feelings. The reverse is not true. There is a need to fuel infatuation. It is self-combustible. But love is fueled by acting lovingly.

Two people standing as a *WE*, acting lovingly toward each other, is an unstoppable force. They stand together, fueling their love by their actions, giving no room for disconnection or doubt. They know where they stand, and they reinforce their stance by acting with love and respect.

It's a simple formula (which does not mean it is easy to implement) that will carry a couple through a lifetime, married and happy.

(You can listen to my interview with Bob Grant about Adrenaline/Endorphin Attraction here: https://savethemarriage.com/bobgrant)

CHAPTER 3.

THE TRAJECTORY OF CONNECTION

"All happy families resemble one another; each unhappy family is unhappy in its own way."
Leo Tolstoy

At least in terms of marriage, I am going to have to disagree with Tolstoy. Unhappy marriages arrive at unhappiness in nearly identical (and predictable) ways. The details may vary just a bit, but the overall pattern is disconcertingly similar.

While marriages each have their unique problems and characteristics, all relationships follow a pattern of connection, and many marriages follow a similar pattern of disconnection. It is this pattern that is so predictable from situation to situation. If your marriage is in trouble, your relationship will likely be reflected in this very pattern of coming together and falling apart.

Let's look a bit at the process of both coming together and falling apart.

One important point to understand is that the process of dissolution of the relationship, if a marriage goes in that direction, is a mirror image of the process of connecting. In other words, in the reverse way you came together, you fall apart, unless you escape the downward trajectory.

Here is a map of that process. We will examine the details below.

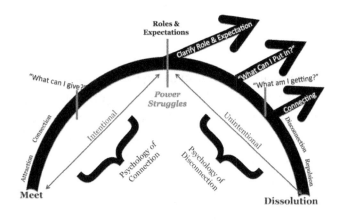

The Psychology of Connection

Let's look first at the growth of a relationship, the Psychology of Connection. Every couple first meets as individuals. For whatever reasons, there is an initial attraction between those two individuals. Somehow, both have a mutual attraction to traits in the other. Perhaps it is appearance or outward personality. Perhaps it is interests or aspirations. And there are certainly some unconscious factors involved. Whatever the reasons for the attraction, they "click."

From that point, each works to build the connection. Each asks the question, "What can I give to this relationship?" This creates a growing connection between the two that feeds off of the connections that each is working to establish. It is a cyclical process of growing and expanding connection. At this point, the relationship is self-nurturing and snowballs into "falling in love." The feeling of connection overflows to a feeling of love and passion. This process is intentional, meaning that both people are intentional about working to connect with the other.

At some point, every relationship, once connected, must find its rules and roles. Two people can only float around in the connecting phase for so long before there has to be some establishment of how the couple will get through life. What are the roles that each will play? What are the expectations that each has for the relationship and the other person? This inevitably leads to some level of struggle, as each attempts to define him/herself, the other person, and the relationship.

Each person is trying to be the one to set the parameters. Not necessarily without input from the other, but headed in the direction desired by each individual. Which causes the struggle.

There is a decision to be made at this point: "Do we come together as a team, or do we continue to struggle?"

If a couple can become a team, a *WE* (which I describe in detail elsewhere in this book), they can escape the other side of the process, the Psychology of Disconnection.

When does the power struggle start? The answer varies from couple to couple. Sometimes, it is early on in the relationship (and continues for a long time for some couples). For other couples, it does not start until the early days of marriage. It is hard to avoid the struggle and negotiation, though, for very long into a marriage. It is hard to be in such an intimate relationship without defining the expectations and roles. It just happens naturally.

(Notice that "naturally" is a different word than "struggle-free." The process can be difficult and full of struggle. I describe the entire process in my Save

The Marriage System, where I discuss the process of discovering true intimacy.)

The Psychology of Disconnection

On the downward side of the arc, we find the process of a relationship when it does not escape the trajectory. This is the process of disconnecting.

In my work with premarital counseling of couples, I notice that without exception, people marry because they want to show their love for the other person. They want to spend their lives expressing this love and being in connection with the other person. Along with the strong element of wanting the other person in their lives, there is the movement of energy toward the other person.

Interestingly, when couples come to my office with a marriage in trouble, a shift has happened. Instead of looking for how they can love the other person, each person is looking for how their spouse is loving them. In other words, the energy has reversed. The prior focus of "How can I love you?" shifts to focusing on "How are you loving me?" This focus quickly shifts to "What am I getting out of this?"

One of the Relationship Coaches in my organization told me that his marriage was deeply troubled, but was transformed when he stopped asking "What am I getting?" and started asking "What can I give?" The shift allowed him to reconnect and reach out toward his spouse again.

There is a built-in scarcity mindset that comes from the perspective of "What am I getting?" The question gets us to focus on lack: lack of love, lack of attention, lack of energy, lack of time, lack of care, etc., etc., etc. What we focus upon, we will find evidence to support — even if that "evidence" exists more in our mind than reality.

"What can I give?" is a question of potentiality. It assumes there is an endless amount of love and affection, which a couple can share together, when that is the focus.

You will notice that asking the question, "What can I give?" is the second exit point from the downward and unconscious trajectory toward dissolution. The question only comes when one or the other person makes a conscious choice to shift.

If the couple does not make that shift, the next level is a growing sense of disconnection. At this point, either or both can make a choice to reconnect, to nurture the connection between the two. This conscious choice to reconnect moves the couple back to a sense of connection, of being a *WE*, and they can again escape the trajectory.

At each point of potential escape, the effort and energy required to escape the trajectory grows.

"Gravity" takes over and accelerates the momentum of the disconnection. Minor issues require minor readjustments. Major issues require major readjustments.

As the disconnection grows, so do the chances for separation, affairs, divorce, and abandonment. The need for connection is so strong that a sense of desperation to find it somewhere grows stronger and stronger.

The human need for connection is similar to the human need for nourishment. If we don't get enough food, anything edible begins to be inviting. Junk food or snacks can start to replace real meals. And desperate enough, humans will consume trash or even dirt to avoid starvation. Starving for attention is no different. The need will be met, in healthy or unhealthy ways.

And as this process of disconnection continues, it leads to the opposite of attraction: repulsion. The person who once attracted the other becomes the object of repulsion. Instead of the "rose-colored glasses" that many wear in the process of falling in love, there are "dark-colored glasses." These glasses only show the negative elements of the other person, dimming the good and positive aspects. Just as we are selective in looking at the positive during the process of falling in love, we become selective in looking at the negative when the disconnection moves to repulsion.

At this point in the process, relationships can still recover. But the energy to do so is far more substantial than earlier in the process. It requires more time, energy, and understanding to turn the relationship back.

The spiral up and the spiral down are mirror images of each other, both moving faster at the ends. Which means that maintaining a connected relationship is easier to manage than is recovery. But recovery is possible all the way to the end of the arc.

Here's a little secret: we all want that connection. And many times, when one can manage an internal shift toward a spouse, the spouse responds, due to this internal desire for that connection. Our drive and need for connection is what allows reconnection. And that reconnection can lead to healing and health in the relationship.

(Excerpted from How To Save Your Marriage In 3 Simple Steps.)

CHAPTER 4.

THE PAUSE-BUTTON MARRIAGE

It happens innocently and understandably. But it happens.

A couple marries and begins to settle into life. Regular life. Not the whirlwind life of love and romance that marked their courtship. Not the excitement of nuptial planning and celebration. But life.

Life begins to return to normal — albeit a "new normal" of marriage and commitment. They love each other and enjoy each other's company. They make plans for the future and move forward together. But now, they do it having made a commitment to be there, to stay in the relationship. No need to chase, no need to try and hold tight to one another. The couple has each other and has promised to be with each other, for life.

This commitment is what allows a couple to relax into the relationship. You make your vows and promises. You commit. You are done with the chasing. I even overheard a bride comment at the wedding reception dinner, "Now I can eat whatever I want. I don't have to worry. You can't leave me. I can just let myself go!" While you might not let yourself go, you get her point. She was seeing her dating days as over. No more winning over, no more worries about losing love. You have your spouse... you have each other... for life.

And so, life starts (or resumes). Married life is the "new normal."

And other areas of life start calling (again).

There are goals to conquer, mountains to climb, kids to raise, friends to see, opportunities to pursue. In other words, there are things to do, people to see, places to go.

Life happens.

And then... the couple hits the "Pause Button." They both think, "As soon as life slows down a little, we will get back to US."

And their marriage becomes the *Pause Button Marriage*.

Except that there is no pause button for marriages.

I've heard the reasoning over and over before. They often have to do with time and energy:

- "Once the kids are older and off to school/off to college/launched in their jobs, we will get back to US."
- "Once I get my career going/get the promotion/get my degree, we will get back to US."
- "Once I run the marathon/climb the mountains/travel the world/accomplish a certain level, we will get back to US."
- "Once we have the house we want/enough money in the bank/retirement secured, we will get back to US."
- Etc., etc., etc.

Whatever the cause of the *pause*, the effect is the same. The marriage is placed on pause... at least that is what the couple (or one spouse) believes.

Except, there is no pause. Relationships are either growing or receding. They can't be paused.

When relationships are paused, they stagnate and recede.

You can probably see it in your non-marriage relationships. Maybe you have a friend that you just know will be for life. But over time, other things get in the way. You don't see each other as much. You don't keep each other updated. And the longer it goes between connections, the easier it is to not connect. Sure, you can "catch up" with each other. But if you don't nurture it, over time, the connection falters.

There is a difference, though, between what happens in marriage and between friends. Between friends, when the relationship wanes, you may miss them, and it may even be a bit painful (especially if you were not the one who backed away). But when it happens in a marriage, the pain is acute, and the need for connection becomes desperate.

Remember, humans are connecting creatures. We are not designed to be solitary individuals but in relationship with others. That need is built into our DNA. You can see it from birth when a child wants contact and connection with parents. At first, the contact is physical — a baby wants to be held and cuddled, changed and fed. And that contact creates bonding. A parent and child bond together.

Plenty of research shows that when children are denied that bond, there is significant psychological damage and pain, some of which can be lifelong. Because humans are designed for that connection and bonding.

Later in life, marriage becomes the vehicle for that connection. And it creates a bond between the couple. The connection nurtures the bond. It allows people to face tough times (and enjoy good times) more than if there were no connection.

Have you ever noticed how sad it is to have something great happen and have nobody to share it with? Or how painful it is to have something tough happen and have nobody to face it with you, to have nobody in your corner?

That connection is built into us. The need for the bond is part of being human. Which is why the *WE* of a marriage is so powerful. It is based in a promise, a commitment, to stay together, through thick and thin, good and bad times, for the rest of your life. And that promise lets you bond more deeply than in any other relationship.

And it also makes any loss of connection ever more painful than any other relationship.

Think of the bond, the *WE*, as the body of the relationship. Think of connection as the lifeblood of that body. And consider what happens when the circulation of blood is disrupted in any organism. The body begins to fail. Health begins to suffer. Pain and discomfort is the result. And left long enough, desperation comes in.

If you hold someone underwater, you see how they struggle to get oxygen (PLEASE do not really try this! Just consider it a thought experiment). At first, it isn't too bad. We can all hold our breath for a bit. But then, it becomes uncomfortable. And then, it becomes desperate.

We are desperate to keep the lifeblood moving and oxygenated.

The *Pause Button Marriage* means that the circulation of connection is compromised. At first, it just feels frustrating and annoying. You might try to get some extra connection with children, colleagues, fellow hobbyists, or others. But over time, the bond begins to fail. The *WE* begins to falter.

Fast-forward to that moment when it happens... the kids are off, the career is made, the goal is achieved. And you turn back to the relationship, press *Un-Pause*, and discover that the connection is gone.

Or as often happens, one person is continuing to move through life, assuming all is good with the pause, but the spouse is feeling the pain and is ready to exit the relationship — or has even found someone else to substitute for the connection!

As benignly as it starts, the Pause Button Marriage claims more relationships than any other single event. In fact, many of those "events," including infidelity, are symptoms of the disconnection that was the unwitting result of hitting the pause button.

Sadly, this is not an intentional action. People don't hit *Pause*, expecting to come back to a relationship on life support. They are "doing life," knowing that the marriage will be there later. They are following passions, dreams, and goals.

But since they aren't chasing those passions, dreams, and goals as a team, the individuals keep moving apart, growing in different directions.

To be clear, there is nothing wrong with having different hobbies and interests, even different friends. The problem is the disconnection. You don't have to be carbon copies of each other. You can order different things at the restaurant, have different interests, enjoy different activities, AND be happily married.

As long as the relationship gets the attention it needs.

As long as you both see yourselves as being on the same team.

As long as you bring the energy from your outside activities into the relationship. You cheer each other on, support each other's goals and dreams... and make some goals and dreams together.

Your individuality is what attracted you to each other in the beginning. It doesn't have to go away to make the relationship work. And you don't have to hit pause to be an individual. You are two individuals, joined together as a unit. The unit part is what can't be paused.

There IS no Pause Button for a marriage.

CHAPTER 5.

WHAT EVERY COUPLE SHOULD KNOW

There are some things that I believe every married person (or anyone considering marriage) should know. Call them basic truths about marriage. Or call them secrets of marriage (because so many people seem to not know these truths). Either way, they are essential to happy marriages. When you don't know them, you often end up fighting against the truths of marriage.

Consider this an abbreviation of the other sections of this book, as quick reminders. It serves as a quick overview that brings everything together for you to see the fit. Use the points as reminders of where to move toward, as well as warnings of why marriages often struggle.

1) Every marriage has difficulties.

Many people are surprised and alarmed when their marriage hits a tough spot. They didn't expect any difficulties along the way. The fact is, every marriage has difficulties.

According to statistics, around 50% of marriages figure out how to deal with the struggles. They realize the struggle is just a part of being that close to someone. When your lives are that intertwined, there is going to be friction.

Having difficulties does not mean the marriage is wrong. It is just a fact of relationships and relating. The real problem is when the issues are not addressed and solved for the betterment of the marriage.

When difficulties are the symptom of power struggles and are not used to grow and form the relationship, they begin to undercut the connection. The difficulties serve to sever the relationship. Instead of being a fact, they are a liability and serve to hurt. Difficulties are a fact, a given. How you face and solve them is a choice.

2) There is no "Pause Button" on relationships.

As I have stated in another chapter, but want to remind you in this short list, there really is no such thing as "pause" in any relationship. Many couples think that they can hit "pause," raise the kids, get the promotions, pursue hobbies and interests, and then return to the marriage down the road. They think their relationship will go into suspended animation.

The connection is the lifeblood of relationships. When you hit pause, you are disconnecting, whether you mean to or not. Connection either grows or recedes. It is never stationary. Many couples "un-pause," only to discover they are disconnected, have grown apart, and are different people. Marriages (and any connection) need regular and consistent care, nurturing the connection and the relationship along the way.

3) Your task is to create a WE

You start every relationship as "You and Me." But marriage is unique. Your task is to become a *WE*, a team, a united sense of yourselves. It's the ability to see that "*WE* are in this together," "*WE* move forward as a unit," "*WE* make decisions on what is best for the US." That sense of being a *WE* is the sign of a successful marriage.

But it still has to have two "Me's" bringing their best selves to the *WE*. A *WE* is not about a "mind-meld" of losing yourself, your identity, to the relationship. It is bringing your best self, your full self, to the team. It is devoting your own individual talents, your individuality, to the best for the team. You are still YOU, just as a part of a *WE*.

If you build a *WE* and focus on growing that *WE*, you have a solid, rock-steady relationship with your partner.

4) Any conflict should be in the service of progress

It is very easy to get trapped in a "win/lose" mentality about conflicts. That is how we respond as individuals protecting our own space. I fight to defend me. You fight to defend you. That is how individuals react to perceived threats. The danger, though, is carrying that over into important relationships, including marriage.

When either person (or both people) is out to win, the relationship loses. Defending ME is often at the cost of *WE*. And is certainly at the cost of defending *WE*.

When couples use conflicts as an opportunity to grow the relationship and build a *WE*, then the conflict is in the service of progress. If you want to win — and try to "score points" in the conflict — the connection gets chipped away, and the *WE* is hurt.

See conflict as an opportunity to progress the relationship. Use conflicts as opportunities to practice being a *WE*. Use them as opportunities to learn about your partner's opinions, about the differences between you, and how those differences can be bridged for the betterment of the partnership. Work to resolve rather than to win.

Work for solutions that move you toward *WE*.

5) *Love is an action. The feeling follows.*

We all love that "in love" feeling. But notice that even in the beginning, actions are what grew the emotions. That never stops. Many people enter into a marriage wanting to show the other person how much they love them. But at some point, many make a shift to asking, "How are you loving me?" This can quickly build resentment – since no one is perfect at showing love. If the question is, "What am I getting out of this?", the marriage will struggle. If the question is, "What can I put into this?", the marriage grows, the connection grows, and the *WE* grows stronger.

Marital love, just to be clear, is not devoid of feelings. It is simply not waiting for the feelings to show up. Love is consistently acting in love. The feelings of love follow up on the actions of love. The feeling of love is from an abundance of connection. Connection is fueled by loving action and nurture.

Simply put, when people wait to feel love before acting lovingly, the feeling continues to diminish, reducing the loving actions. And the spiral continues downward... away from action and feeling. But choosing to act lovingly builds the feeling. Which does make it easier to act, which leads to a deepening feeling. And the spiral continues upward.

Action leads to feeling. Don't wait for feelings in order to act. Act and watch the feelings come (or strengthen, once you have the momentum shifted).

When we struggle against these truths, it's like swimming against the current. Sure, you might be able to do it for a while. But it is both tiring and ineffective. You might hang on for a while. But eventually, exhaustion and frustration set in. And if you keep it up, you never get to your destination. You give up and head for shore.

But if you follow these truths, you are swimming with the current, making even faster progress than swimming in still water. You might just enjoy the journey! Let the current help you out!

CHAPTER 6.

INFIDELITY AND OTHER SYMPTOMS

I'm asked the question on a regular basis: "My spouse had an affair (or I had an affair), so that is the real issue in our marriage, right?"

The answer is "No."

It is like saying, "I have a fever, which is making me feel bad. That is the problem, right?" That is actually a symptom. The underlying reason for the fever is important. Sure, you can take something to break the fever. But that doesn't mean you are well. You just eliminated a symptom.

The underlying infection is the real problem that must be addressed. The fever is just the body's response to the underlying issue. It is a symptom, not a cause.

Infidelity is a symptom of the marital crisis. It isn't the cause. But like a fever, the symptom can cause extensive damage, so it is not just an irrelevant issue.

The problem is that infidelity often makes one spouse the target — the "fault" of the marital problems. The focus on the one who had the affair means that the real issue can be ignored or denied. And in the process, the underlying issue cannot be addressed or healed.

Let's be clear: Infidelity is damaging to the relationship. One person ventured out of the bounds of the relationship, rupturing the boundaries of the relationship. In its wake, damage is done to both people. And there is extensive damage to the relationship.

The spouse who suffers the affair feels a disruption of trust and confidence. They have a hard time trusting the relationship or the spouse. They lose confidence in themselves for being an adequate spouse and for being able to provide what is needed in the marriage (since the spouse who committed the affair ventured beyond the marriage for those needs). And they struggle to understand who their spouse is, given those actions.

The spouse who commits infidelity has likely rationalized why such behavior is acceptable, since such behavior usually challenges their moral stance. Shame (unless thoroughly rationalized away) is often an underlying feeling. But then there is that connection with the affair partner... it acts almost like a drug. The person committing the affair may try to pull back, pull away from the affair partner, only to go back for yet another "hit" of the intoxicating connection.

Infatuation, fueled by the dynamics of the affair, is often confused with love, with proclamations that "I've never felt this way before," a belief associated with every instance of infatuation. (We tend to do a poor job of remembering the depths and power of prior emotional moments — accurate memories of all powerful emotional states are suspect, be it the depths of pain or heights of joy.)

But because of the overwhelming feeling of infatuation, the person who committed the affair confuses that feeling with proof that the relationship is "right." And the justification continues.

And the damage is done.

In reality, the affair is only the "presenting problem." In a medical office, patients come in with "presenting problems," but they are really symptoms of a bigger problem. A fever is the symptom of an infection. An upset stomach, headache, fever, chills, and a sore throat are the presenting problems, often symptoms of the flu. The issue driving the symptoms, the infection, is what needs treatment. If successfully treated, the symptoms abate as the infection abates.

So, what is the underlying issue with affairs?

Disconnection and Infidelity

As we discussed earlier, the need and desire for connection is wired into our DNA. It is part of being human. We need and crave closeness (even if the closeness scares us — the mirror fears of abandonment and intimacy).

That closeness is critical for well-being. If it isn't in our lives, we go searching for it. We may not recognize it in the search, but that is what we are trying to find. Connection, closeness, intimacy with someone.

In our culture, that means connection with "that one," the "soulmate" that fulfills our physical, emotional, and spiritual levels of connection. And when that connection wanes in one relationship, it may be found in another. If a marriage does not hold the connection, another relationship may emerge.

But disconnection is not all that is necessary. It is just the vulnerability. It sets the stage.

There's a problem: connection is not a consistent reality. In every single marriage, the level of connection can vary over time and circumstances. And one person can feel closer or more distant than the other person. In other words, connection — the feeling of connection — is a subjective reality. I can feel closer to you than you feel toward me, and vice versa.

Maybe it is a busy time at work, or the kids are pulling at you. We all only have so much energy. That is also part of being human. There is a limit to our energy reserves that we can invest anywhere. If some area of life needs more attention, another area of life will pay the price. I only have so many eggs to put in all the baskets of life. If one basket needs more eggs, they are coming out of another basket.

Disconnection in a marriage is not a conscious choice, by the way. It happens in the small decisions and choices, some of which, at least, seem to be unavoidable. We have some circumstance that seem to demand attention, and so, we pull some energy from somewhere else... like the marriage.

Marriage is often taken for granted. After all, we did pledge to stick together for life, right? Yes, but we forget that when we make that choice, we are also committing to making the relationship a priority. But if our lives don't reflect the prioritization, the marriage begins to be the source of energy that is moved to other areas of life.

The Eisenhower Matrix (made famous by Stephen Covey) notes that we tend to ignore the non-urgent but important areas of life, ceding them to *urgent/important* and *urgent/unimportant* areas of life. Marriage is — until it is in crisis — an *important/non-urgent* area of life. Sure, we know it is important, but many people think it will be there, safe and secure. And so, energy that should go there is funneled to other areas of life that *seem* to need immediate energy (some do, and some don't).

And the connection in the marriage begins to recede. When energy is pulled from one area of life, that area simply has less energy than it had before.

Which leads to that Arc of Disconnection. The less connected we are, the less we feel the need or desire to connect. And the less we connect, the more we disconnect... unless we do something to shift the dynamic. Unless we go from *unconscious disconnecting* to *conscious connecting*.

But if connection ebbs and flows in every relationship, does that mean that every marriage is at risk?

At risk, yes.

Yet, not every marriage suffers infidelity.

Why?

Because of the other factor — boundaries.

Boundaries and Marriage

Connection is the energy within the relationship (or lack of energy in disconnection). Boundaries are the borders of the relationship, protecting it from outside forces. In some ways, it forms the "skin" of the relationship, a barrier to the outside world.

Boundaries are what individuals do to protect the relationship from outside forces. You can also think of them like the moat and walls around the castle. While life goes on inside the building, it is protected by the moat and walls, so life is safe.

Every marriage needs boundaries. Many do not have stated or agreed upon boundaries, though. How do I know? Because I have asked.

In pre-marital counseling, I have asked couples to think through their boundaries — how they will agree to protect their relationship. Almost always, this has not occurred to them, since they believe their love will keep them safe (it won't).

At marriage enrichment events, I have asked couples who are doing okay about the boundaries. They haven't agreed to boundaries — and it feels strange to have that conversation when things are okay... why rock the boat? (Except that the relationship needs those boundaries for those disconnected times.)

And in my work with marriages on the edge of failure, it is almost always the case that boundaries are absent (or very blurry). In fact, had there been boundaries, infidelity would not be an issue.

My task here is not so much to tell you how to set your boundaries, as much as point to the fact that it is a factor in affairs. It is what allows infidelity to creep into a relationship. (Mostly because the boundaries do not keep the emotional energy from creeping out of the relationship.)

Boundaries are best when agreed upon by a couple. When both commit to the boundaries, it is much more likely to be effective than when one person decides to inflict boundaries upon another person — often, when connection simply cannot sustain such a demand.

Best practice would be for a couple to set and agree to boundaries before they ever enter into the marriage. In reality, this does not happen often. Leaving the marriage vulnerable.

Appropriate boundaries clarify what each person does to protect a relationship — interactions with outside people, verbally, emotionally, and physically. For example, what is okay to share with others? What are situations that would be considered risky for outside interactions? What types of interaction are reserved for a spouse? Answers to those simple questions can clarify and secure the marriage before it gets into trouble.

But when those answers are not known, we humans tend to do one thing very well: rationalize. We do an excellent job of making the "gray areas" of life acceptable and even reasonable.

Disconnection + Lack of Boundaries = Vulnerability to Infidelity

Let me be clear, just because there is disconnection and there are no clear boundaries, that does not mean infidelity is inevitable. Only that there is a high vulnerability to infidelity.

When disconnection comes to a relationship — and it comes to every relationship, to some degree — one or the other may seek some sense of connection somewhere. They may find it by throwing themselves into work, friendships, parenting, pets, or other points of contact. (To be clear, involvement in work, friendships, parenting, etc., is not necessarily a sign of disconnection. But it can be used as a substitution for marital connection.)

We have already noted that humans are built for connection. There is a secondary fact: we are also designed for attraction. We tend to notice other attractive people, and even have a physical response of arousal to other people. That is just part of human wiring. The question is not whether people might feel attraction, but what they might do about it.

I've never been to a wedding where the couple pledged to never, ever notice another human being again — to never be attracted to anyone else again. But they do usually vow to "forsake all others." In other words, they pledge to not allow others to get too close and pledge to not get too close to others.

Which is where boundaries come in. Those boundaries are the protection points of the relationship. It is the "arm's length" that couples agree to keep others that might otherwise interlope into the relationship.

When both factors happen, disconnection and a lack of boundaries, the marriage is vulnerable to infidelity.

Conversely, when couples have strong boundaries, the relationship can weather the points of disconnection that may emerge. That gives the couple a safe space and the time to reconnect. A connected marriage with strong boundaries has a low risk of infidelity.

Can A Marriage Be Saved AFTER Infidelity?

Clearly, infidelity is an assault on the *WE*. It is damaging to both the one who suffers and the one who commits the infidelity, and it is damaging to the relationship.

It is not, however, necessarily the end of the marriage. While statistics are a bit hard to come by around the topic of infidelity, what research we do have reflects that a slight majority of marriages that suffer infidelity do survive.

In my experience, for many marriages, infidelity can actually serve as an eye-opener, a "wake up call." It causes the couple to face the issues and problems present in their marriage. They are forced to face the disconnection and unhappiness that have been a part of the marriage. And they have to decide upon either working through the issues or walking away.

Granted, it is best for a marriage to not suffer infidelity, to learn about the disconnection in a less bruising and hurtful way. But if infidelity occurs, it is possible to learn the lesson and recover.

Once they can recognize infidelity as a symptom of the hurting marriage, then the focus is not on the affair, but on the marital relationship.

At this point, let me be very clear here: The person who commits infidelity is 100% responsible for having taken that action. Whether there was disconnection or not, whether there were boundaries or not, committing the act of infidelity is 100% the responsibility of the person who did it. Blaming a spouse is not appropriate, nor is hiding behind the disconnection as an excuse.

But both people are fully responsible for having been a part of a disconnected marriage. Both people have to "own up" to their role in that disconnection. And both are responsible for the efforts to rebuild the connection.

The person who committed infidelity, though, also has the responsibility of re-establishing trust. It is on that person to be transparent and accountable — the beginning point of re-establishing both trust and boundaries.

How to heal after an affair is beyond the scope of this particular book. It is, however, the subject of my book, *Recovering From The Affair:*
http://viewBook.at/recover-from-affair.

CHAPTER 7.

Q&A

Over the years, I have received questions from people in similar situations as you. Many times, they were the same questions. I can guess some of the questions you may have at this point. They are likely to be similar to the questions from thousands of people who have already asked them of me. So, allow me to ask and answer those questions for you.

If my marriage is in trouble, can it be turned around?

The short answer is yes, it *can* be turned around. Statistics back me up on this one. For couples with whom I work directly, my approach has worked with near 80% effectiveness. So we know the approach I use works.

That said, the real question you are asking is "*will* my marriage turn around?" Statistics are rather irrelevant, except for how they play out in your life.

And that is harder to answer. Yes, it can be turned around, but will it be turned around?

There are several dynamics that play into this. Some are within your control. Some are not.

First, beyond your current control is the *timeframe* of the crisis. Simply put, the longer the disconnection and crisis, the harder it is to shift back. The damage mounts up. Crisis becomes chronic.

Also beyond your control are the *actions* of your spouse. Some spouses either refuse to reconsider or even add to the damage by the actions they take.

But there are some things you do control. You can decide that you will make the necessary changes to get things back on track. You can act on that decision, making the changes. And you can continue to act on that decision, often despite the actions of your spouse, to hold the changes you made. All of that is within your control.

To make it as simple as possible, saving a marriage has three steps. They are simple (but that does not mean they are easy). I call them the "3 C's" in my book, *How To Save Your Marriage In 3 Simple Steps*. Here they are:

- **_Connect_ with your spouse (given the disconnection that got you here).**

- ***Change* yourself (given the fact that we all have places to improve and change).**
- ***Create* a new path (given that most marriages never found the WE path).**

When connection is re-established, it is like restoring circulation to the body — barring too much damage, it comes back to life! And the only way to know is by trying. If something happens to me, I do hope the medical staff will at least try to restore my circulation (CPR, defibrillation, etc.) before they decide nothing can be done!

It's the same with a marriage. Yes, your marriage *can* be turned around. *WILL* it be turned around? There is only one way to find out... *TRY*.

But what if my spouse doesn't want to?

First, if BOTH of you wanted to turn it around, with the right approach, you are pretty much unstoppable! Since your approach hasn't been helpful up to this point, you do need a new one. But given a new approach to your relationship, you and your spouse can absolutely turn it around.

But second, and this is a missed point in so many methodologies, one person can choose to start the process... even if a spouse is refusing to try.

I have long made my approach usable and effective with one person deciding to work on the marriage. In fact, the byline of my *Save The Marriage System* is that you can save your marriage, "even if only you want to."

But many people say, "it takes two to have a marriage."

They are correct.

Long-term, it does take two people to have a great marriage, both invested and working on it.

BUT, and it is a big "but," it only takes one to start the process. And isn't that true in anything in life?

One person starts the movement. One person might even take the lead in moving in a different direction.

A thought always starts with one person. That one person can take actions, even if others haven't yet started acting — or even accepted — moving toward a given goal.

Think of marriage like a dance. You two have been dancing for a long time. Your steps are coordinated with each other. But not necessarily to the music. In other words, you have been out of step with the goals of marriage, but in step with each other. You move, your spouse moves. Your spouse moves, you move.

What if one person changes the steps... even a little? The spouse has to change their steps, too. Otherwise, you aren't dancing anymore. And marriage is the dance.

In a relationship, if one changes, the other changes. Kind of like a math equation. You have to change both sides of the equation. And to be honest, this is how the marriage got so far off course. You kept (often unknowingly) following each other down a dead-end path.

Now, you have the option to take the lead, to change the steps. And at some point, your spouse can join in that new dance. And in most cases, they do.

It does "take two to tango." But it only takes one to ask the other to dance, and even to lead the dance.

"I just want to get back to where we were, though. Can't we just do that?"

In a word, No.

For a longer response, where you were got you to where you are. A marriage crisis is a good indication that your approach and your process are not healthy and helpful for your marriage.

Your current situation is rooted in the dynamics and understandings of your marriage. So, just going back to where you were will get you right back to where you are.

Fortunately, making a shift is not hard. It is more a realization of what wasn't right and shifting to what is a better path.

But what if we just stay for "the wrong reasons?"

Lots of marriages get to the right place because they stay for the wrong reasons — in the beginning.

Whatever reason for staying, if it keeps you together in order to get to the right place, then the reason gives you the opportunity.

The problem is that people think in binary terms: left/right, up/down, right/wrong. And in marriage crises, that often amounts to two choices:

1. Stay in the marriage and be miserable.

2. Leave the marriage and be happy.

Missing is what I call "*The Third Option.*" In almost every situation, there is a third option. In marriage, it is:

3. Stay married and make it a relationship BOTH treasure and protect.

Granted, many have a very hard time even visualizing that third option. But it IS there, waiting to be grabbed.

So, if there is a reason that keeps you there long enough to get to option #3, that works (unless the reason is coercion or force). If you decide to hang in there for the kids, because you don't want to give up assets, or because you don't have the finances for two households, count it as an opportunity to move toward a third option.

Some research shows that unhappy couples who simply hang in there for two to three years report being happier. Without therapy or any other intervention. Simply by hanging in there.

So, hang in there!

"When Is It Unrecoverable?"

Let's first be clear that there is a difference between *unrecoverable* and *unrecovered*. Many marriages could be recovered. But that does not mean they will be recovered. Some couples mutually choose to walk away. In that case, not much can or will happen. If neither has a desire to work on it, little will shift.

Other times, a spouse wants to save the marriage, but simply does not know what to do nor how to do it. In those cases, the loss of a marriage is more about lack of knowledge than lack of desire. The solution is to find a helpful approach to the marital issues. (That was one big reason I created the *Save The Marriage System*. I wanted to solve the problem of people not knowing how to save their marriage.)

And there are still other times when one person in the marriage simply will not make a shift, regardless of what you do. They are closed to the possibility and opportunity to rebuild a marriage. This is the true tragedy. A recoverable marriage, except that one person refuses.

When I sit with couples where one wanted in and one wanted out, I am quite clear that a marriage requires a unanimous vote to stay together, but a single veto could end it. That is the reality of our "no fault" divorce laws. These laws are, in actuality, "single party initiated" divorce laws. It simply does not require both people to want it. Which means that one spouse has control of the dissolution of a marriage, like it or not.

As I noted in the introduction, the other type of marriage that I do not think should be recovered is the abusive marriage. It is beyond the scope of this resource to tell you whether or not your marriage is abusive. If there is physical violence, though, it is abusive. If you are still reading, despite my words in the introduction, please get help. That is not a marriage that should be recovered.

Beyond an abusive marriage that should not be saved and the times when a spouse simply will not allow it to be saved, most situations are recoverable.

Oh, and if your spouse seems to be refusing now, do not assume that this situation cannot be changed. We change our minds all the time, on a myriad of things. And that includes wanting out of a marriage.

While I was a chaplain, I watched people as they faced low odds of survival. When presented with some way of beating it, some way of finding a cure, almost all went for it. They didn't pause to say, "If you can guarantee I will be cured, I will do it." They turned it around and said, "If there is a chance of a cure, I will do it. Let's see what happens!"

There is one way to find out whether or not your marriage can be recovered: work toward restoring it. Not haphazardly, but with a plan that is effective. Find the resources that show you how to work on it. And then, work on it.

"Why Even Try?"

That is a great question. Perhaps you are reading this information more as a post-mortem. Perhaps you are interested in what killed your marriage, not how to revive it. I get that.

A marriage crisis can be overwhelming and painful. You may just be searching for information to help your understanding and processing. In that case, trying is simply not on your agenda.

So just to reiterate what I said above: if neither of you wants to work on it, nothing will happen. Sure, the divorce can be painful. But if both of you have accepted the reality of it, you are simply moving through the pain.

But what if that is not you? What if you wanted to diagnose the problem *so that* you could move forward and restore the marriage? Should you? Why should you?

First, I will tell you that it is my conviction and belief that a bonding happens in a marriage that is more painful to pull apart than any other relationship — even when the marriage has had pain, conflict, contention, fighting, and arguing. It is still pulling apart a relationship that was based on a promise for life.

Which is why a divorce is considered to be one of the most stressful events in life.

But more than that, a good marriage is one of the best buffers to the other stressors in life. If you have someone you can count on (and vice versa), you can stand together through the tough times life holds. Two are much stronger than one, when they stand together as a unit, a *WE*.

Over the years, I have discovered the fact that marriages which have weathered a tough marital time and come out together on the other side are stronger and more resilient as they move forward. Taking on tough marital times and allowing that to strengthen your relationship means you are more resilient for all the other tough times in life. And I did mention (didn't I?) that 100% of marriages have difficult times. The task is holding on, making it through, and getting to the other side with a stronger relationship.

Also, let's talk about the kids (even if the "kids" are adults). A divorce absolutely does affect the children in a family. I have seen it for myself (personally and clinically), and research backs it up.

A few weeks back, I had a parent tell me that the kids would be fine. I agreed that the kids could certainly recover (not would... but could). But that is not the same as saying they will be fine. This person told me that a psychologist said it was better for a child to have divorced parents than deeply conflicted parents. I told him that he was choosing between worse situations — basically trying to decide which bad situation was better.

I asked, "Which do you think would be better for a child? Fighting parents, divorced parents, or happily married parents?" He grudgingly agreed that under any situation, a child would be better off with happily married parents.

When parents show their kids a happy marriage, they learn some critical lessons. Like the importance of commitment. Like the value of working through tough times. What love really looks like. And they have a sense of stability in their own lives.

Emotional well-being of the spouses, emotional well-being of the children (and other family members). Those are two great reasons to work on it.

Not to mention the negative financial consequences, the resulting mess of taking things apart, the jigsaw puzzle of schedules with kids — including holidays and schools, and the loss of time with the children that each spouse endures, along with the children involved.

Oh, and the big surprise for divorced spouses with children... they are forever connected together, anyway, because of the kids. They are, by necessity, forced to relate and coordinate with each other for life (or refuse to do so and cause more emotional damage to the children). The same issues are still present unless you at least solve the issues between you.

So at least do that.

But guess what? If you can solve your issues, you can restore your marriage.

I can't make you want your marriage. I can't convince you to work on your marriage. But I can provide the resources and guidance you need, IF you decide you want to do that.

"How Can I Get My Spouse Into Therapy?"

There is a simple question to ask before you even try: *Should* you get your marriage (and your spouse) into therapy?

Let me be clear: there are some excellent marital therapists out there. They do excellent work with couples, and they can help your marriage.

Elsewhere, I have already noted the rather dismal statistics around marital therapy. Now, let me tell you the reasons why those statistics are so bad. One has to do with therapists. The other has to do with clients.

Therapist Problem: Remember when I noted that a "Systems" approach to thinking about marriages and families shifted me during college? I began to see the family as a web of relationships affecting each other. Which is a departure from individual psychology, looking at the intrapsychic issues of people.

This is where it matters: any therapist can claim to be a marital therapist. Regardless of training. And many individual therapists decide to also see couples — but they do not make a shift in their method. They end up approaching the relationship as if it is just two individuals involved. That approach is both inaccurate and unhelpful (if not destructive).

Capable marital therapists are trained as, well, marital therapist. Their graduate training should be as a marital and family therapist. Be sure and ask about that.

Client Problems: There are a couple of problems that clients bring into the session, which can also hamper progress, if not cause deeper issues.

The first problem, and it is a major one, is dragging a resistant spouse into therapy. To say that more clearly, for therapy to work, BOTH of you need to be willing and ready to address your problems. If you want therapy to help you heal your marriage, you both need to be ready to work on your relationship.

I can't say this strongly enough. If your spouse does not want to go to therapy and does not want to work on the marriage, do not try to coerce them. You will only find yourself with a more resistant spouse, more convinced that the marriage is doomed. They practically convince themselves of that in therapy, as they attempt to convince you and the therapist of the same.

The second problem is how you use the session. Many couples decide to simply use it as a venue for fighting... presumably with a "judge" (the therapist) to decide who is right and who is wrong. Deep within all of us, we want vindication. We want someone to say, "this isn't your fault." And we tend to draw others into the drama, in the hopes of finding a favorable judgment. A therapist is not a judge. And therapy is not helpful as a venue of judgment.

If you are asking the question, "How can I get my spouse to go to marital therapy?", please note that you likely have a resistant spouse (otherwise, they would be in agreement to go to therapy). If you get them there, you would want to make sure you found the right therapist. And then, you would need to make good use of the sessions. All are tall orders when you start with a spouse who is dragging their feet about therapy.

"How Can I Get Help, Then?"

It is interesting for me to often go through the statistics of therapy, explain why therapy is an issue, and then be asked about a recommendation for a therapist. It tells me that we, as a culture, are deeply therapized and psychologized. We automatically go to therapy as the help.

And it can be, with the right therapist and the ready spouse. But it can be destructive if your spouse is not ready and the therapist is not right.

Does that mean you are out of luck? No. There are other sources of help:

Coaching: As opposed to therapy (in marital therapy, you need both people), coaching can be done with only one person — the one wanting help.

In fact, I do that type of coaching, and have a trained team of coaches, working with clients when only one spouse wants to work on things. (We also work with couples, when both are ready to get their marriage on-track.)

Retreats: Sometimes, a spouse will not be willing to go to therapy, believing it would be too intimate a space. But they are willing to go on a marriage retreat. There are good retreats and bad retreats, though. You want to check out any retreat, making sure you agree with their methods and theories.

Workshops: These marriage workshops are often held by organizations that provide excellent training and tools for couples to use and solve their own issues. And again, you want to make sure you agree with method and theory.

Online courses or books: These resources are easily accessible and can be effective. You do want to make sure the approach you choose is legitimate and not manipulative. But since there is no travel involved, they are affordable and easy to access.

Quite frankly, this is why I created the *Save The Marriage System* and why I wrote the books. I wanted to put the tools and knowledge into the hands of people who are ready to get going. One note: be sure you are using information from someone who is trained and experienced. Just because someone saved their own marriage, that does not make them an expert in saving your marriage. Nor is someone with an opinion, but lacking in true experience or training.

Remember this: if your spouse is not ready, you can still start acting. You can start the process, begin to change your approach, and let the relationship start to shift.

And if you need some help in assessing potential help, I created a resource on *Getting Help For Your Marriage*. I tell you how to assess a therapist, to see if one might be a good fit, as well as how to best use other methods of getting help.

You can get that resource right here
GETTING HELP FOR YOUR MARRIAGE :
https://savethemarriage.com/gethelp

"But When Did This All Start?"

First, let me say that I understand why you might ask this question. But second, I want to be clear that this question is rarely helpful. It gets us turned in the wrong direction. It turns you back to the past. It is about what has already happened. And what cannot be changed.

Throughout this resource, I have tried to explain why marriages get into trouble. Dynamically, the way they get into trouble is similar across all hurting marriages. The specifics may vary from couple to couple. But the underlying issues are incredibly consistent.

And the crisis builds slowly. Which means that finding the specific point of origin is pretty much useless and impossible.

When you learn the dynamics at play, you can often look back and see the places that the principles apply You can see the way those dynamics are playing out in your own relationship. Which is different than finding the starting point. You are simply highlighting how those dynamics are playing out in your relationship.

The question, "How did we get here?" is natural. But it is better to decide, "Here we are." And then ask the question, "Now what?"

You do need to understand the dynamics involved. And then you need to find an approach that fixes the underlying dynamics, bringing healing and connection back into the relationship.

Let's talk some about resources that may help you with help in the next chapter.

CHAPTER 8.

WHAT NOW?

My goal in this book was to point out and highlight why marriages get into trouble. To go one step further, I have outlined why marriages fail and end in divorce. If you are like me, you are concerned on a macro-level about how many divorces happen in our culture. My concern is about how many of those divorces are unnecessary.

But that leads to your specific concern — how to keep your own marriage from ending in divorce.

We have discussed the fact that marriages get into trouble when the connection that sustains a relationship falters and fails. That is often because people struggle with becoming a WE, either because they lack the knowledge, or they have fears that keep them from stepping in. And often, it is a matter of having hit the "pause button." People just don't realize that relationships can't be paused — but they try, anyway.

And we now know that the disconnection can lead to hurtful situations, including infidelity. We looked at how affairs are not the cause, but a symptom of the marital issues. Certainly, infidelity can multiply the issues in a struggling marriage. But affairs more highlight the disconnection that is present (and the boundaries that are missing) in the marriage.

This book was designed to help you understand "what happened?" But the next question, the one that ultimately changes things, is "what now?"

Back in college, I enjoyed my class in anthropology and archeology. It was interesting to learn about what we can discover from digging up old artifacts. We can surmise how a civilization came to be... and how it crumbled. History is certainly informative and can be entertaining. And it can *help* us decide how we want to proceed. But in the end, any archeology site is only digging up dead stuff. Life left long ago.

Don't get caught in the "archeology dig" of your marriage. Lean toward engineering... building something. Once you know what went wrong, you can move forward differently. You can build the marriage you want and desire.

You *can* move forward. The question is whether you *will*.

Which starts with you.

You stand at a fork in the path. My guess is that either you or your spouse have already decided that going down the same path you have been on — unhappily married — is not an option. One or both of you may be seriously considering the fork that heads toward divorce and dissolution. But don't be fooled into thinking that is an easy or painless path. Nor should you believe it is the only available path.

The other fork in the path takes you to a marriage you both would treasure, enjoy, and protect. It may be a very faint path from here... barely discernible. And that is the thing: the path to divorce is well-trodden. Plenty of people have walked right on down it, not knowing there was another option. And culture lines that path, making it seem clear and simple (not helpful, healthy, or healing... but clear).

While you may not be able to see so clearly down the other path, that fork toward a healed and healthy marriage, it is there. It is a choice. And I would argue that it is a better choice.

But only you can choose which fork to take.

I would like to just point to some of my other resources that can be helpful to you, if you choose that fork.

Podcast - *The Save The Marriage Podcast*: This free podcast gives you lots of resources to help you in your efforts. I cover the full range of marital crises, from early stages to late in the game. As of publication of this book, there are well over 250 episodes for you to access and listen. To access the Save The Marriage Podcast, go here: http://SaveTheMarriage.com/stmblog or search for it on your favorite podcast app.

Book - *How To Save Your Marriage In 3 Simple Steps*: This book describes my 3-step process for saving a marriage — the 3 C's. Just to be clear, "simple" should not be confused with "easy." But in this book, I show you that saving a marriage is not complicated. While there is effort involved, you need to only focus on three areas. If you are overwhelmed and confused, let's simplify and break it down, so you know what to do. Go here to find it : (http://getbook.at/3ss.

Book - *Recovering From The Affair*: This book gives you a path to healing after infidelity, whether it was physical or emotional, and whether you committed or suffered the affair. I discuss the reasons behind infidelity, the power of an affair, and the process of recovering from an affair. The book is designed for couples to use, either individually or together. Go here to find it: http://viewBook.at/recover-from-affair .

Online Program - *The Save The Marriage System*: This virtual program has been used by almost 100,000 people around the world, over the last two decades, to save and rebuild their marriage. It is designed to be used by one person, even if that person is the only one who wants to save the marriage. Many have said that the core module should be read by anyone getting married. And it has been instrumental in many marriages being restored and improved. Since it is a digital program, it can be accessed from anywhere in the world, from just about any device. Go here to find it: http://Save TheMarriage.com.

The resources are there, waiting for you. The help is available. In addition to the listed resources, I have a staff of coaches, all ready to help. I have a community of people who are doing exactly what you are doing.

The starting point, though, is you. All the resources in the world are useless without your first step. Your marriage *can* be saved.

Will it? The way to find out is to get started.

I wish you well on your journey to save and restore your marriage, making it a relationship that both you and your spouse will protect and treasure.

And now, it is YOUR move....

ABOUT THE AUTHOR

Lee Baucom is the author and creator of many books and programs. After training as a therapist, Lee continued his training in life coaching. He is an expert in the area of relationships and thriving.

The host of two podcasts, Dr. Baucom provides help, coaching, and training to people around the world. His efforts have allowed many people to rebuild their marriages. And with his resources, many people have found their purpose in life. He has helped marriages and individuals to thrive.

In addition to his coaching and writing, Dr. Baucom is Co-Principal of a worldwide coach training program. His efforts allow people to transition to coaching careers, working as positive impactors in the world.

Happily married for over three decades, Lee is also the father of two adult children.

In his spare time, Lee enjoys trail running, paddle boarding, scuba diving, and jiu jitsu training.

Find out more at amazon.com/author/Lee-H.-Baucom-Ph.D.

Or visit http://leebaucom.com

OTHER RESOURCES
BY LEE H. BAUCOM, PH.D.

BOOKS:

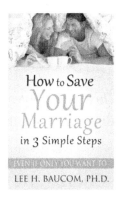

How to Save Your Marriage In 3 Simple Steps
http://getbook.at/3ss

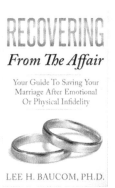

Recovering from The Affair
http://viewBook.at/recover-from-affair

Thrive Principles
http://TheThrivePrinciples.com

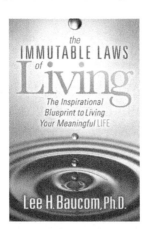

The Immutable Laws of Living
http://TheImmutableLawsOfLiving.com

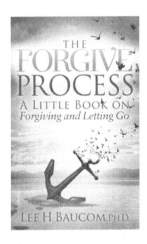

The Forgive Process
http://TheForgiveProcess.com

PODCASTS:

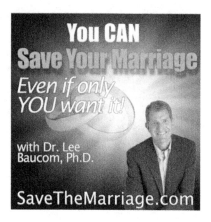

The Save The Marriage Podcast
http://SaveTheMarriage.com/stmblog

The Thriveology Podcast
http://ThriveologyPodcast.com

CAN I ASK A FAVOR?

If you enjoyed this book, found it useful or otherwise, then I'd really appreciate it if you would post a short review on Amazon. I do read all the reviews personally so that I can continually write what people are wanting.

If you'd like to leave a review, then return to where you got the book.

Thanks for your support!

Made in the USA
Middletown, DE
30 June 2022